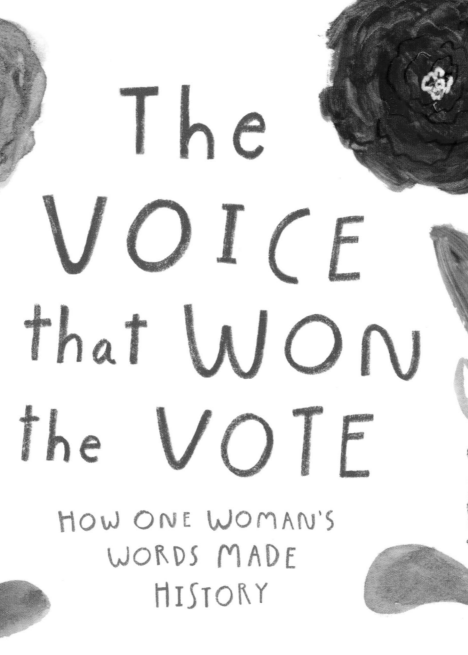

The VOICE that WON the VOTE

HOW ONE WOMAN'S WORDS MADE HISTORY

Elisa Boxer

ILLUSTRATED by
Vivien MILDENBERGER

PUBLISHED by SLEEPING BEAR PRESS

A vote is a voice:

This is what I believe in.

This is what I stand for.

This is what matters to me.

This is who I am.

This is who I choose to lead
my town, my state, my country.

In 1920, women were still denied that voice.

For nearly seventy-five years, they had organized meetings...

Marched in parades...

Carried signs...

And made speeches, demanding their right to vote.

"Say yes to suffrage!"
they shouted.

They wore yellow roses.
"Yellow means yes!"

But they were silenced.
Other voices drowned them out:

"Troublemakers!"

"Uncivilized!"

"Female voters will surely cause chaos!"

"Women with a voice in politics? Nonsense!"

"The only vote a woman needs is the vote to choose her husband!"

But nestled in a valley, on a farm in East Tennessee,
one woman was determined to have a voice.

And a vote.

Febb Burn was known around town as smart and strong-willed. At a time when most women didn't go to college, Febb did. She graduated and became a teacher. She read newspapers, magazines, and books. She loved to learn.

Febb Burn was especially fascinated by laws and the people who made them.

Every year, on election day, the men who worked on her farm would head to town hall to cast their votes.

And every year, Febb Burn would watch them go.

She was sick and tired of staying home, shut out of the process.

So one day, she sat on her front porch with some paper, a pen, and a plan.

"Dear Son," she began . . .

A few days later, a letter arrived on the desk of the youngest lawmaker in Tennessee.

His name was Harry Burn. And on that hot August day, he watched the state capitol fill up with reporters, photographers, and people from all over the country who had come to witness history.

America was on the verge of change.

Thirty-five states wanted women to vote.
But the country needed thirty-six to make it law.

It all came down to Tennessee, the last state left to vote.

If lawmakers in Tennessee said "yes," women across the
nation would finally be allowed to cast their ballots.

If Tennessee lawmakers said "no"?
Well, things would stay exactly the same.

It was a tie.

They would have to vote again.

Harry Burn was ready to stand firm for what he believed in.
He had voted against women's suffrage in the first round.
He knew that most of the people who had elected him hated
the idea of women voting. Many of those people were in the
audience. They knew they could count on Harry Burn.

After all, the proof was right there on his jacket: a red rose.
The symbol of keeping women in the home, and out of the
voting booth. The State Capitol was filled with more red roses
than yellow that day, and everyone knew what that meant.
Someone would break the tie with a "no."

It was time to vote again.

Someone did indeed break the tie.

Harry Burn.

"YES," he said.

What? The officials in charge asked the young lawmaker to repeat himself.

Obviously, he'd made a mistake.
Clearly, he'd gotten confused.

But there was no mistake.
He was not confused.

Harry Burn wanted women to vote!

No one could believe it.

Many of the women who had organized meetings,
marched in parades, carried signs, and made speeches
were in the audience wearing their yellow roses.

They gasped and cried and hugged each other.

But why did Harry Burn change his vote?

"I know that a mother's advice is always safest for a boy to follow," he explained. And then, from his jacket pocket, behind that red rose, Harry Burn pulled out a note.

From his mother.

The one Febb Burn had written on her front porch.

Hurrah and vote for Suffrage and dont keep them in doubt. Dont forget to be a good boy.

With lots of love, mama

The people who had elected Harry Burn were shocked. And furious.
A grown man listening to his mother?

We'll show him, they thought. We will NOT
vote for Harry Burn in the next election!

"Burn Ruined in Politics!" declared the headlines.

Harry Burn understood.

He knew that by giving women the right to vote, he was giving up his seat in the Tennessee House of Representatives. The people in his district just weren't ready for a leader who wanted women to vote.

He told newspaper reporters, "I am happy simply because I followed my conscience. It kept telling me women are people."

And voting, he knew, should be the right of all people.

He thought again of his mother.

"So I made the choice," he said, explaining that standing up for what he believed in was more important than winning the next election.

It took courage.
And courage has a way of making things right.

Election day came.

When the campaigns were over and the votes were counted, the new state representative was announced:

Harry Burn!

He kept his seat in the Tennessee legislature,
kept standing up for equal rights.

And no one was prouder
than the woman who, without speaking a word,
gave all women a voice.

The moment Harry Burn cast his tie-breaking vote for women's suffrage, he came under fierce attack from his fellow lawmakers. They accused him of everything from being a traitor to taking bribes. His political enemies couldn't accept how he had listened to his heart over public opinion. He had to hire a bodyguard because his opponents tried to attack him. They tried to get him to change his vote. They tried to get his mother to negate her letter.

But Harry Burn, like his mother, didn't let the loud voices of others drown out that quiet inner voice that let him know what was true. Part of what drew me to this little-known story was the fact that Harry and his mother both made a major impact on history by trusting their truth and speaking out for the oppressed.

In defending his vote for suffrage, Harry Burn wrote in the legislative record that he wanted "...to free seventeen million women from political slavery." In fact, the women's suffrage movement had its roots in the anti-slavery movement. When people began holding meetings to talk about ending slavery, many women were prevented from speaking out about it. Women were still considered the legal property of their husbands and fathers, with no rights of their own.

In their fight for a voice in freeing the slaves, women began to recognize their own inequality, and the importance of changing that. So the early suffrage movement was as much about freeing women to be in charge of their own choices, voices, and lives, as it was about freeing them to be in charge of their own ballots.

Selected Significant Events in the Women's Suffrage Movement

1848
The Seneca Falls Convention. The nation's first women's rights convention, held in Seneca Falls, New York, results in a document called the "Declaration of Sentiments." It calls for equal treatment of women, including the right to vote.

1872
Activist Susan B. Anthony is arrested for trying to vote in New York. She's convicted of voting illegally and fined $100. She refuses to pay.

1887
The first women's suffrage amendment comes up for a vote in the U.S. Senate. It is defeated.

1890
Wyoming becomes the first state to grant women the right to vote.

It took courage for Febb Burn to express herself in that letter, telling her son Harry that she wanted him to "...vote for suffrage and don't keep them in doubt." The illustration of Febb's letter features her actual words. It also took courage for Harry to change his vote from "Nay" to "Aye." (Those were the words used in the legislature back then. I have used "No" and "Yes" in this book for clarity.)

I hope this story inspires you to find similar courage to express what's in your heart and trust your inner voice, even when it goes against the louder voices around you.

I want to share with you one of my favorite ironies in the tale of the Tennessee vote. On that hot August day in 1920, House Speaker Seth Walker listened to his fellow legislators speaking for and against women's suffrage. When he was confident that his side had enough votes to keep women out of the voting booth, he stood up on the House floor and called for the historic vote.

"The hour has come," he said. "The battle has been fought and won."

He was right, of course. Just not in the way he assumed. The hour had come for those who had been silenced to finally have a voice. May you never forget the power of yours, to express what matters to you.

For an educational guide and photos of Febb's letter, please visit sleepingbearpress.com/teaching_guides.

1916
Activist Alice Paul and her colleagues form the National Woman's Party to fight for women's suffrage. They organize parades, rallies, petitions, and speaking tours to protest the fact that women can't vote.

1917
The National Woman's Party becomes the first group to picket the White House. Known as the "Silent Sentinels," the protestors stand outside the gates with signs and banners, trying to persuade President Woodrow Wilson to change his mind and support suffrage. Many are arrested on charges of obstructing traffic. Others are attacked by anti-suffragists and by authorities.

1919
The U.S. Senate and House of Representatives pass the Nineteenth Amendment to the Constitution, allowing women to vote. But 36 states have to ratify it before it can take effect.

1920
The Nineteenth Amendment to the Constitution is signed into law, guaranteeing all American women the right to vote. The Amendment reads: "The right of citizens of the United States to vote shall not be denied or abridged by the United States or by any State on account of sex. Congress shall have power to enforce this article by appropriate legislation."

For Evan. May you always know how much your voice matters.
And for the silenced. May you still find a way to speak.

Elisa

to Marliese, a guiding voice I can always rely on.

Vivien

With deep gratitude to my editor, Sarah Rockett, and the entire team at Sleeping Bear Press, for sharing my vision and championing this book into the world. I couldn't ask for a more supportive team as a debut author. To my agent, Steven Chudney: thank you for believing in me and for the heads-up about the 100th anniversary of the Nineteenth Amendment, which led me to dig up this story. To Vivien Mildenberger: I am in awe of how beautifully you brought my words to life. To Kyle Hovious, in Special Collections at the University of Tennessee Libraries, Knoxville: thank you for your research assistance. And to my trusty beta reader, Evan: I'm so grateful for you. It's no coincidence that my first book centers around a mother's extraordinary bond with her son.

Photo courtesy Tyler Boyd (great-great-grandson of Febb Burn) on behalf of the Burn family

Printed and bound in the United States.
10 9 8 7 6 5 4 3 2 1

Library of Congress Cataloging-in-Publication Data
Names: Boxer, Elisa, author | Mildenberger, Vivien, illustrator.
Title: The voice that won the vote : how one woman's words made history /
By Elisa Boxer ; Illustrated by Vivien Mildenberger.
Description: Ann Abor, Michigan : Sleeping Bear Press, [2020] | Audience:
Ages 6-10 | Summary: "Women's suffrage in America came down to a single
voter in Tennessee who voted yes because of a letter his mother had
written, urging "Vote for suffrage and don't forget to be a good boy."
This is the story of the letter than gave all American women a voice"-- Provided by publisher.
Identifiers: LCCN 2019047089 | ISBN 9781534110496 (hardcover)
Subjects: LCSH: Suffrage--United States--History--20th century--Juvenile literature. |
Women--Suffrage--United States--Juvenile literature. | United States. Voting Rights Act of 1965.
Classification: LCC JK1846 .B69 2020 | DDC 324.6/230973--dc23
LC record available at https://lccn.loc.gov/2019047089